AQUARIUS

JANUARY 22–FEBRUARY 19

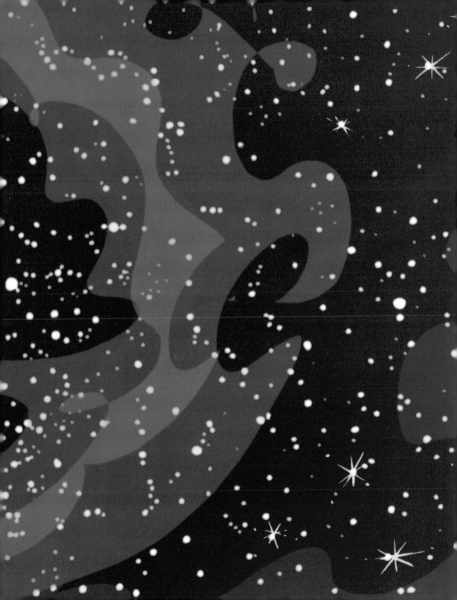

· JUNIOR ASTROLOGER ·

AQUARIUS
JANUARY 22–FEBRUARY 19

ALEXIS QUINLAN

ILLUSTRATIONS BY IRENE ROFHEART PIGOTT

CADER BOOKS · NEW YORK

Andrews and McMeel
Kansas City

Editorial: Jackie Kramer, Jake Morrissey, Dorothy O'Brien,
Regan Brown, Nora Donaghy
Design: Charles Kreloff
Copy Editing/Proofing: Garet Scott
Production: Carol Coe, Traci Bertz, Cathy Kirkland
Legal: Renee Schwartz, Esq.

Printed in China.

If you would like to share any thoughts about this book, or are interested in other
books by us, please write to: Cader Books, 38 E. 29 Street, New York, NY 10016.

Or visit our web site: http://www.caderbooks.com

Library of Congress Catalog Card Number: 96-79243

June 1997

First Edition

10 9 8 7 6 5 4 3 2 1

Attention Schools and Businesses: Andrews and McMeel books are available for
educational, business, or sales promotional use. For information, please write to:
Special Sales Department, Andrews and McMeel, 4520 Main Street,
Kansas City, Missouri 64111.

TO KATE PARRISH
SHOCK JOCK
SISTER,
AND FRIEND

CONTENTS

Psst!
Looking for
predictions? Sorry.
The best astrologers
know that the stars don't
make things happen—
people do! (But if you
must have your
fortune told, turn
to page 64.)

WELCOME TO ZODIAC ZONE

Imagine our world without skyscrapers, highways, or malls to block the horizon. Imagine our planet without flashing signs or neon lights to compete with the brightness above. It's just you and the great sky: the fiery sun blazing above every day, the moody moon changing its shape all month long, and the glittery planets and stars bedazzling the sky every night.

That's how it was 5,000 years ago, in the ancient city of Babylon. There, in the cradle of civilization, the very first stargazers sat atop zigzag-shaped towers, called ziggurats, and invented a system to make sense of the stars.

In the beginning, astronomy (the simple study of the stars) and astrology (the study of the stars' influence on people) were the same thing. That's because the Babylonians—along with the Indians, Chinese, and Native Americans—believed in something called Cosmic Sympathy. They thought that the universe, or cosmos, was so perfectly arranged that every single part was connected to every other part. The Greeks described this link between heaven and Earth best when they said: "As Above, So Below."

This philosophy led stargazers to look for connections within the heavenly hodgepodge of the sky.

The ancients played connect-the-dots with the stars and "drew" favorite animals and legendary heroes onto the sky. And so the constellations were born. As people continued to watch the sky and record what they saw, they noticed that each spring the constellations were in the same positions they'd been in the previous spring. The same was true for summer, fall, and winter—the movement of the constellations was completely in tune with the seasons. In this way, the stars provided the first calendar, useful for recording important events, planting crops, and keeping holidays. And because of their belief in Cosmic Sympathy, these early people thought that the constellations themselves were powerful—that the stars brought the seasons with them as they shifted across the heavens. The most important of these constellations were the twelve that make up the zodiac: the narrow belt of stars through which the sun, moon, and planets seem to move.

The word "zodiac" comes from the ancient Greek word for "circle of animals."

11

The first stargazers believed that the sun, moon, and planets were powerful, too, and so they named these heavenly bodies after their mighty gods. Kings and queens appointed astrologers to observe planetary movements and translate their messages. These sky watchers looked for special astral events like eclipses, when the moon seemed to gobble up the sun, or bright spots, when two planets passed just next to each other. They would use these omens, or signs, to tell their leaders whether it was a good day to go into battle, to start work on a new building, or to stay home and nap. Over the years astrologers began using the movements in the sky to learn more about regular people—not just royalty. They found that people born at the same time of year—when the sun is in the same position in the sky—have a lot in common. This gave rise to sun-sign astrology—the same kind of astrology you often see today in newspapers and magazines.

The word "planet" comes from the ancient Greek word for "wanderer."

Of course, nowadays astronomy is a science entirely separate from astrology. But astrologers continue to be fascinated by the possible connections between what happens in the

12

sky and what happens in our lives here on Earth.

This brings us round to you, dear reader. When you were born, the sun was in the sign of Aquarius. The sun, being by far the brightest, hottest, most amazing thing in the sky, stands for your natural gifts—the things you can do while walking backward and chewing gum. It also shows your will—the way you work for what you want.

The fascinating world of astrology can help you make the most of your gifts and talents, strengthen your weak spots, and lead you to a whole lot of fun. But as you ramble through the zodiac zone, remember: The stars are what you make of them. There are as many different types of Aquarians as there are Aquarians, and you'll always be one of a kind!

HERE'S YOUR MAP

When you were born, the sun, moon, and planets were arranged in a special pattern along the zodiac. A horoscope (one of an astrologer's tools) is a map of the sky pattern at a specific point in time. Because the sun, moon, and planets are always moving at their own speeds, and because the Earth is always spinning, the horoscope changes all the time. (The word "horoscope" comes from the Greek words for "watcher" of the "hour.")

We couldn't include your personal horoscope (because everyone's is different), but you can see

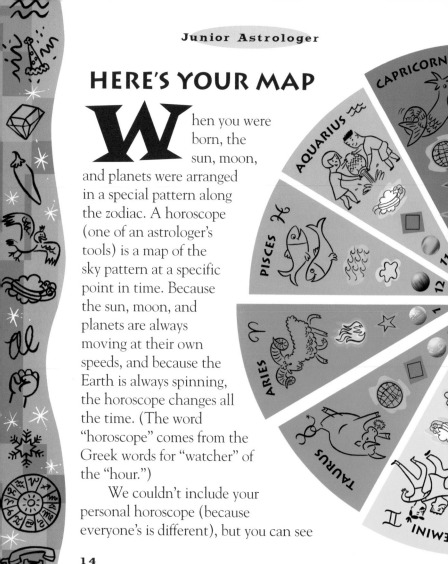

14

where your sun sign falls along the great wheel of the zodiac. Each section shows a sun sign and its name, glyph (a special squiggly mark that stands for the sign), symbol, element, quality, ruling planet, and order in the zodiac—all stuff you'll find out about in this book.

**To figure out people's
sun signs, look up their
birth dates below:**
Aries: Mar. 21–Apr. 20
Taurus: Apr. 21–May 20
Gemini: May 21–June 20
Cancer: June 21–July 22
Leo: July 23–Aug. 23
Virgo: Aug. 24–Sept. 22
Libra: Sept. 23–Oct. 23
Scorpio: Oct. 24–Nov. 23
Sagittarius: Nov. 24–Dec. 22
Capricorn: Dec. 23–Jan 21
Aquarius: Jan. 22–Feb. 19
Pisces: Feb. 20–Mar. 20

THE MOON AND PLANETS

Like the sun, the rest of the solar system also influences parts of your character. Think of these heavenly bodies as one big, happy family that's always near to back you up.

FEELINGS: Matched by most ancient cultures with family and the night, caring Mother **MOON** watches over your moods and emotions.

COMMUNICATION: Named after the fast-talking Roman messenger god, Brother **MERCURY** encourages you to express yourself.

BEAUTY: Named for the Roman goddess of love and pleasure, charming Sister **VENUS** shares her great taste in clothes, food, and art.

POWER: Named after the Roman god of war, Brother **MARS** teaches you to stand up for yourself. He inspires you with ambition and energy.

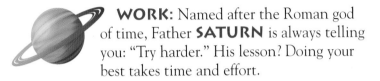

ATTITUDE: Named after the Roman leader of the gods, jovial Uncle **JUPITER** looks at the bright side of life. He reminds you to keep your chin up.

WORK: Named after the Roman god of time, Father **SATURN** is always telling you: "Try harder." His lesson? Doing your best takes time and effort.

IDEAS: Named after the Greek god of the sky, Uncle **URANUS** loves your wild brainstorms. Just look up, and he reminds you: "The sky's the limit!"

DREAMS: Named after the Roman god of the seas, Aunt **NEPTUNE** splashes her magic around. She encourages you to dive into your imagination.

UNDERSTANDING: Named after the Greek god of the underworld, Great-Uncle **PLUTO** is deep. His sensitive smarts help you figure things out.

17

IT'S ELEMENTARY

Long ago, people thought the world was made of just four elements: fire, earth, air, and water. Though we now know our planet has more than a hundred elements, these first four elements are still astrology's building blocks. In the zodiac, elements stand for personality types.

FIRE SIGNS are energetic, eager, and proud. Aries, Leos, and Sadges head straight for the action—spreading warmth along the way.

EARTH SIGNS are no-nonsense, trustworthy, and successful. Tauruses, Virgos, and Caps make dreams come down-to-earth true.

AIR SIGNS are cool, idealistic, and social. Geminis, Libras, and Aquarians follow the breeze to fun and friendship.

WATER SIGNS are caring, artistic, and slightly psychic. Cancers, Scorpios, and Pisces figure out any situation they dive into.

YOUR STAR QUALITY

That's right, every sign has a quality, too: cardinal, fixed, or mutable. A quality relates to the season in which it appears, and it stands for a sign's behavior style. Each sign has a different combination of elements and qualities.

CARDINAL SIGNS begin the seasons. No wonder Aries, Cancers, Libras, and Caps are bursting with creativity. Sometimes pushy, often independent, always ambitious— cardinal kids get noticed.

FIXED SIGNS are cozied up in the middle of a season. That must be why fixed kids are steady, stubborn achievers. Tauruses, Leos, Scorps, and Aquarians never give up on projects or pals.

MUTABLE SIGNS show up when seasons change. Count on Geminis, Virgos, Sadges, and Pisces to be resourceful and flexible. Mutable kids might change directions a lot, but their eyes are always on the prize.

AQUARIUS IN MYTHOLOGY

The symbol of Aquarius has always been a boy carrying an urn. Some say the boy was Ganymede, cupbearer to the king of the gods. When he wasn't serving nectar to Zeus, he poured heavenly knowledge to earth.

There is another myth about Aquarius. One day Zeus saw that people had become cruel and selfish, so he decided to destroy them all in a flood. But one man named Deucalion heard the news, and he built a wooden box for himself and his wife, Pyrrha. After a nine-day downpour, the couple was washed ashore on Mount Parnassus. They hurried to the magical oracle, or wise man, to ask how to bring back the human race. The oracle said to wear veils on their heads and toss stones over their shoulders as they walked. The rocks Pyrrha threw became women and Deucalion's rocks became men. Then they started a new kingdom full of generosity and good will.

BEING AN AQUARIUS

Welcome to the Age of Aquarius! If you're born under the ultimate air sign, you're the Shock Jock of the airwaves. Famed for friendliness and genius, you broadcast brainstorms across the zodiac. As a fixed-quality kid, you're stubborn about your bright ideas: You want the whole world to share them!

Your glyph is the waves of wisdom poured to help humankind. Or is it lightning bolts? Your helpful notions can be electric!

Your ruler is Uranus, the Roman sky god. Called the Great Awakener, Uranus fills you with shake-'em-up ideas. Before Uranus was spotted (back in 1936) your ruler was Saturn, the wise old god of discipline.

Your star challenge? Even Aquarius kids can't live on ideas alone. Sometimes, you're so busy chasing rainbows that you forget homework, friends, and even food!

Astral advice: New pals are always spinning into your orbit: slow down to enjoy them!

21

ABSOLUTELY AQUARIUS

The zodiac is rich with thousands of years of history, myths, and legends. Each sign has a treasure chest of colors, gems, foods, and more. Here's what's special to (or ruled by) Aquarius.

MOTTOS: I Know; I Understand

RULING PLANET: Uranus

COLORS: Sky blue, all electric colors

GEMS: Aquamarine, black pearl, sapphire

STONE: Obsidian

METAL: Aluminum

BODY AREAS: Ankles, calves, shins

NUMBER: 4

DAY: Saturday

FOODS: Souffles

VEGETABLES: Jalapeño and Serrano peppers

FRUIT: Dried apricot, kiwi, lime, raisin, star fruit

FLOWERS AND PLANTS: Elderberry, frankincense, orchid, violet, all fruit trees

ANIMALS: Eagle, all big birds that fly far

CITIES: Bremen and Hamburg, Germany; Brighton, England; Moscow and Saint Petersburg, Russia; Palo Alto, California

COUNTRIES: Iran, Israel, Poland, Russia, Sweden

NATURE SPOT: Vineyards

AQUARIUS ALSO RULES: Airplanes, astrology, clubs, electricity, hopes, ideals, light bulbs, psychology, radio and TV announcers, telephones, TV sets, stereos, surprise parties, anything brand new.

Measuring Up Rulers: In astrology, every sun sign has one ruling planet that keeps an eye out for the sign and protects it. In turn, each sun sign rules many people, places, and things.

YOUR KIND OF AQUARIUS

Like any circle, the zodiac has 360 degrees—giving each of the twelve signs 30 of those degrees. Each sign is further divided into three 10-degree subsigns. These are a combination of the sign with another sign in its element. Which means there are actually three different kinds of Aquarius.

All three subsigns remain friendly Aquarians, the Shock Jocks of the zodiac, but each one has a slightly different style and goal. Just as Aquarius has a ruler—Uranus—Aquarius subrulers come from the air signs of Aquarius, Gemini, and Libra. Knowing your subsign helps you make the most of your special talents.

AQUARIUS-AQUARIUS

AQUARIUS-GEMINI

AQUARIUS-LIBRA

FIRST SUBSIGN: THE AQUARIUS-AQUARIUS
January 21–January 30
Rulers: Uranus-Uranus
Qualities: Fixed-Fixed
The Genius

As a double Aquarius, you soar in the element of ideas. An added dose of Uranus brings bold plans for the future, a love of science and invention, and a wacky sense of humor. Lots of your notions are off the wall, since you're a sci-fi dreamer at heart. Being extra fixed, you go for goals with gale force. After all, you've got news to share, water to pour, a whole world to save! Once you solve a problem, you're bored—that noggin moves at lightning speed. Good thing your body moves quickly, too. You're always ready for the next adventure. Sure, your independence is famous. But you team up like a pro, and you never make fun of other kids. You're a walking recipe for popularity!

SECOND SUBSIGN: AQUARIUS-GEMINI
JANUARY 1–FEBRUARY 9
RULERS: URANUS-MERCURY
QUALITIES: FIXED-MUTABLE
THE SOCIALITE

Just as much of a Shock Jock as your neighbor in the first subsign, your subruler Mercury, (the planet named for the messenger god) means you spread the word as fast as quicksilver. Gemini's the jokester sign—you toss out your wild ideas to pals and watch the arguments explode. The mutable boost keeps you flexible: Forget rigid rules and schedules. You'll try a dozen approaches to any goal, and you reserve the right to change your mind at any time. Your nose for news helps you spy fads and trends months before your buddies. Some friends might tease "Sure, your ideas would work—on Uranus!" But you still manage to talk pals into the weirdest stuff. You always change a group for the better.

THIRD SUBSIGN: THE AQUARIUS-LIBRA
FEBRUARY 10–FEBRUARY 19
RULERS: URANUS-VENUS
QUALITIES: FIXED-CARDINAL
THE ANSWER KID

Your specialty? Smart solutions that make everyone happy. Libra brings a strong sense of fairness, thanks to those scales. You're as likely to change the world as your neighbors in the first two subsigns, only you do it without tipping the balance. Subruler Venus lends a kind, artistic nature, and an eye for the best. You see the best in most everyone you meet, too, which wins you a passel of pals. The dash of cardinal quality means you defend your beliefs like a leader, and you've got the

ambition of a big-shot, too. Finally, you like one-on-one palships more than most Aquarians—Libra is the sign of partnership.

FAMILY MATTERS

Aquarius brings happy laughs, upstart ideas, and great conversation to any family—just ask yours. Family is your very first group, and you're an expert at groups. During dinner, you want the whole clan to share the day's jokes, lessons, and dreams. Sometimes you're so interested that you forget to eat! You aren't wild about chores (although cleaning the refrigerator can be as fun as a science experiment) but you pitch in and give your best, since you'd hate to let the team down.

Check out the sibling and parent starguides to maximize your star power on the home front.

SIBLING STARGUIDE

Powerful as the planets are, birth order is important too. Where do you fall in the family lineup?

OLDEST KID: You're a fair-'n'-square big sib, always ready to take on extra responsibility. You look out for the tots without them ever suspecting! (You want them to have their freedom.)

YOUNGEST KID: As a quick learner, you soak up fun facts from big brothers or sisters. But you never blend in or just follow along. Your quirky independence has the big kids learning from you, too!

MIDDLE KID: It's great to be in the center of it all. And when you go roaming after one of your Day-Glo rainbows, the sibs are always waiting back home.

ONLY KID: A good spot for the free-thinking Aquarius. You absorb parents' news, then head out for adventure. Your birthday bashes are the best, since you invite everyone!

PARENT STARGUIDE

Parents are great, yes, but they are adults. For some stellar help with keeping them happy (and getting what you want), look up your parents' sun-sign below.

THE ARIES PARENT

This parent is bursting with fiery ideas for fun. Thrilling? Always. Tiring? Not for you. Best of all, Ram loves your individuality! When you want a green light, appeal to Aries' weak spot—tell Mom or Pop you'll be first on the block to try it.

THE TAURUS PARENT

Your shenanigans alarm stable Bull. But this parent provides solid ground, and your free spirit always returns home. For special favors, show your fixed determination. Ask two or three times—Taurus likes consistency.

THE GEMINI PARENT

This parent shares your bubbling curiosity, and is at least as interested in your schoolwork as you. For far-out missions, explain strategies to the last detail while cracking jokes. Like you, the Twin can't resist a witty line of logic.

THE CANCER PARENT

A worrier? Maybe, but Cancer loves fretting over home base. A witty imp like you can only please. For that rock-climbing trip, discuss the safety measures and your excellent guide. And always mention "home"—this word is music to Crab's ears.

THE LEO PARENT

The generous fire sign treasures your trademark independence and provides a deluxe home base. But cross the majestic king or queen, and you can expect a dramatic roar! For a royal seal of approval, appeal to Leo's pride in you—it is huge.

31

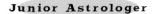

THE VIRGO PARENT

This keen-eyed down-to-earthling sees your potential and wouldn't want you to waste it. Want a big Yes? Let Mom or Pop know how carefully you've thought through your plan. Details are everything with Virgo.

THE LIBRA PARENT

This fellow airhead adores your logic and quirky smarts—you two can discuss anything! Sure, Libra offers a million "what-if's" to every gung-ho plan. But you love knowing all your options.

THE SCORPIO PARENT

You two make a truly fixed family, even if your independence gets squeezed by this super caretaker. Just don't hide motives— Scorp sniffs them out. For favors, play up the mystery. Make like a detective on a mission.

THE SAGITTARIUS PARENT

This parent shares your freedom-loving spirit, applauds your quest for truth, and laughs at all your jokes! No wonder you're a famous pair. When heading for a fresh adventure, appeal to Sagittarius's sky-high optimism.

THE CAPRICORN PARENT

This parent believes in hard work and determination. When your wacky plans have you floating on cloud nine, Cap brings you back to earth. In need? Use the "I've thought long and hard about it" approach.

THE AQUARIUS PARENT

This parent inspires with quirky notions, high-flying ideas, and brilliant flashes. And you're both firm believers in the future. In a jam? Explain to Aquarius the Elder how you were trying to change the world for the better.

THE PISCES PARENT

Congrats, you've won the most indulgent parent in zodiac-ville. But the sea-deep Fish can be shocked by your free-and-breezy ways. For special permission, pour on the syrup—Pisces responds to a little sappiness.

CELESTIAL SCHOOL TIPS

Earth to Aquarius! Yes, astrologers call you a genius, and say you're fifty years ahead of the times. But what about those days the zodiac's absent-minded professor has to be in class?

Check out pointers from the planets. They'll help you rule in school.

PROBLEM SOLVE. It comes easily anyway, thanks to your inborn logic and electric intuition.

ASK QUESTIONS. Use that burning curiosity. New info is rocket fuel for the Shock Jock.

WORK WITH PALS. You can learn from study groups—and they'll surely learn from you.

TAKE NOTES. It keeps you involved.

JUST IMAGINE. No, grades aren't everything. But with a little concentration you can zip to the head of the class!

ASTRO ANGLES FOR SPECIFIC SUBJECTS

SCIENCE: For Aquarius, experiments are a way of life. And the study of the latest technology shoots an easy A your way.

SOCIAL STUDIES: Social minded Shock Jock loves civics. Soon you're suggesting protest marches for class field trips.

ENGLISH: Air signs run communication, so reading and writing come free with the Shock Jock package.

MATH: Problem-solving skills make your math path a downhill glide.

HISTORY: Surprise! This subject can perk up even a far-out future-thinker like you. Tune into inventions and revolutions (both Aquarius-ruled).

LANGUAGES: No culture *shock* here! That gift of gab is your passport.

Special Aquarius Study Tip: You're unique, no doubt about it. Add your special stamp to projects and assignments—you'll love the results (and so will teacher)!

ASTRO ACTIVITIES

You're more famous for exercising your brain than your body. But fun sports, games, and hobbies are a breeze for the ultimate air sign. Your friendliness, fairness, and ability to keep cool make you a natural leader. To make sure an activity is out of this world, ask yourself some key questions:

Is it a little complicated?
Is it a lot of fun?
Are pals involved?

Three yeses make it an Aquarius activity.

SPORTS: Never underestimate the power of a good workout. (It makes use of your electric energy!) Sports fans can expect the unexpected when you're on the field—you take risks! In football, you like a speedy running job rather than blocking or tackling. The hectic soccer field is a real kick for Aquarius. Field hockey is awesome, but baseball and softball are your true loves: there's nothing like a fly ball soaring through the blue sky to make you happy! One-on-one sports like tennis, badminton, and Ping-Pong keep your spirits up. Too, you like the cool purity and precision of ballet and karate. Horseback riding and roller-skating or blading are fantastic—you love the feel of the wind in your face.

ART: There's an awesome artist inside every Water Bearer. Whether painting, dancing, or writing, you lend your special touches or even invent new crafts. You add cool paint or glitter to your model cars, or your dolls might get a new outfit, stitched by you, so they stand out from the other dolls on the block! As an air-sign communicator, don't forget the mighty pen. Writing helps you record your far-out dreams for the future and all the cool things you notice here and now.

HOBBIES: Reading opens magic doors for the Shock Jock; science and science fiction catch your attention first. Mysteries and brainteasers are faves too—no doubt you've invented a few yourself. The curious scientist in you wants to know how things work.

Whether it's from the kitchen, the backyard, or a toy store, Aquarius turns just about anything into an experiment. But your collections of dolls, cards, charms, stickers—and friends—are just for fun!

Sometimes your airhead needs a good airing out! Hit the great outdoors for stargazing, cloud-watching, or exercise—though you're more likely to jog toward town than to the country. And remember, clubs with a cause are second nature to Shock Jock. You want to make a difference, but you don't want to do it alone.

HIGH-TECH DELIGHTS: Radio, TV, and computer games come easily for the Shock Jock. And many say the World Wide Web is the first sign of the age of Aquarius! In any case, you and the Internet are a match made in cyberspace. Your scientific side loves the technology, and you make friends quicker than you can say "on-line!"

STAR STYLE

CLOTHES: No frills please. Sure, you can pull on silver high tops to remind the world of how special you are. But mostly you need room to play.

BEDROOM: There might be a rainbow printed on one wall and a stack of books by your bed. But not too crowded! The ultimate air sign needs room to think.

FOOD: Often confused with science class. Add jelly to chicken and pickles to peanut butter. No experiment is a failure as long as you're learning.

MUSIC: With fixed determination you practice the elegant piano or the laid-back guitar. Why not sing along, too? (You probably have a great voice.)

VIDEOS: Ooey-gooey romances give you the yawns. Go for outerspace adventures, tales of mad scientists, mysteries, and anything that's brand-spanking new.

STAR PETS

Some say people choose pets that remind them of themselves. Is it any surprise that Water Bearer wants a pet with smarts and individuality?

You like a young, frisky pup that you can teach a kennel-load of tricks. A well-trained Labrador retriever or sheep dog is cool (you'd love to help train seeing-eye dogs). Cleaning up isn't your thing, but you don't want your mutt stuck in a mess any more than you want to live in one.

Your fantasy pets are genius dolphins and white Siberian tigers. Freedom-loving, sky-aiming birds capture your airy imagination, although you'd hate to see them in a cage. Even bats and old-time pterodactyls get you going. But carrier pigeons could be the Shock Jock's number one hit—they spread the word fast! Finally, bears are ruled by Aquarius—they're always sniffing around for new experiences!

FRIENDSHIP ALONG THE ZODIAC TRAIL

Friendship is ruled by Aquarius. You're a good mixer—you've got a crowd of pals from school, from scouts, and from the swim team. But you don't follow the crowd. The only thing you follow is your own mind! You happily go off on your own to explore. So how is it that you wind up as a leader so often? Perhaps it's your change-the-world plans, or maybe it's your constant fairness and kindness.

The thing that flattens your airwaves? Clingy people who try to pin you down. Super-cool Aquarius must be free!

One warning: Your strong beliefs can sting some pals. Try to put friendship before philosophy.

On your astro-tour of friendships you'll see that every star combo has its ups and downs. You've got so much to teach and learn from each sign, that any duo can work!

For a smoother ride on the Zodiac Trail, brush up on your planets (page 16), elements (page 18), and qualities (page 19).

ARIES FRIENDS

DATES: MARCH 21–APRIL 20
SIGN OF THE RAM
ELEMENT: FIRE
QUALITY: CARDINAL
RULER: MARS
SYMBOL: THE RAM'S HORNS

First in the zodiac, Aries kids try to come first in everything else, too. Cardinal-fire kids like nothing better than adventure. Ruled by the warrior Mars, they battle for beliefs. These pals are Red-Hot Chili Peppers! Fortunately, Rams cool down as quickly as they flare up.

There's no beating around the bush with this gutsy fire sign. Ram cheers your social smarts and bright ideas, while you're bewitched by this firestarter's action-packed adventures. "Who needs plans?" asks Aries. "Let's go!" And you're cool enough to pretend Aries is in charge.

Star Wars? Aries fights mightily when you disagree—and this pal doesn't mind a noisy melee! Then Ram laughs it off and enrolls you in the next adventure. But this teaches you to stand up for yourself. And in the end, you two inspire each other.

TAURUS FRIENDS

DATES: APRIL 21–MAY 20
SIGN OF THE BULL
ELEMENT: EARTH
QUALITY: FIXED
RULER: VENUS
SYMBOL: THE BULL'S HEAD

The first down-to-earth sign in the zodiac, Taurus's green thumb works magic on plants, projects, and friends. These fixed-quality beasts hardly ever brag, and never start stuff without a clear plan. Ruler Venus lends a love of luxury, a taste for good food, and a laid-back streak. Just call these cuddly kids Teddy Bulls.

Though you're no snob, you admire this fellow fixed kid's quest for the best. In return, your breath-of-fresh-air ideas shake up comfy Taurus, who might be dozing before the TV if you hadn't come knocking!

Star Wars? Couch potato alert! This grounded pal likes to stay put while you're swinging off the edge of a star. Push Taurus, and you get the dread *bull*headedness. (And you thought you were stubborn.) But count on play-it-safe Bull to be loyal at the end of the day.

GEMINI FRIENDS

DATES: MAY 21–JUNE 20
SIGN OF THE TWINS
RULER: MERCURY
ELEMENT: AIR
QUALITY: MUTABLE
SYMBOL: THE ROMAN
NUMERAL TWO

Geminis are shortwave radios. Tune into these restless air signs for insider info, funny jokes, and strange trivia. Thank ruler Mercury, planet of fast talk and fleet feet. The mutable quality makes these sidekicks born jugglers— Twins work best on two projects at once.

Oh, why do you like the fast-moving smooth-talker so much? This playful air-sign pal takes your hand (Gemini rules hands) and drags you from back-yard to playing field. Meanwhile, you inspire Twin to turn that talk into action for a good cause.

Star Wars? The Quicksilver Kid brings news you can use, but the gossip drives you bonkers. And some of those pranks! Egad! But keep this friendship light and airy, and you're guaranteed gobs of giggles.

CANCER FRIENDS

DATES: JUNE 21–JULY 22
SIGN OF THE CRAB
RULER: THE MOON
ELEMENT: WATER
QUALITY: CARDINAL
SYMBOL: THE CRAB'S CLAWS

Cancer's moods might change with the moon, but these lunar (not loony!) types always make sure everyone is happy, safe, and fed. Count on an elephant's memory—straight A's in history—and worrywart ways. Even when Crab seems shy or dreamy, this cardinal sign has goals galore.

The Moonshine Kid uses extra-sensory intuition to build you up. And even though Cancer is sentimental about tradition and old stuff, this pal gets excited about your splendid new ideas, so you're never alone. In exchange, you involve your pal in the latest hubbub. And just watch Crab sink those claws in!

Star Wars? Cancer's watery worries rain on your parade. And Crab can get a little *crab*by. In short, this pal might bug you like family. But, like family, Cancer offers mega-support.

LEO FRIENDS

Dates July 23–August 23
Sign of the Lion
Ruler: The Sun
Element: Fire
Quality: Fixed
Symbol: The lion's
    mane and tail

Leo is just your average king of the jungle—creative, loyal, and dramatic. Sun-ruled Lions take center stage, toss their manes about, and then brag about their big deals. But these fixed-quality kids aren't totally self-centered. Leo rules the heart, after all, and theirs are made of pure gold.

Showtime! You two impress each other with your fixed determination. And the Sunshine Kid is ready to put a fire to your off-the-wall plans. Together you charm your way into many happy hijinks.

Star Wars? No matter how much you share the work on a project, showbizzy Leo takes the glory. And if you accidentally step on the Lion's mane—uh-oh. Good thing this palship is too dandy to let minor mishaps turn into grand grudges.

VIRGO FRIENDS

DATES: AUGUST 24–SEPTEMBER 22
SIGN OF THE MAIDEN
RULER: MERCURY
ELEMENT: EARTH
QUALITY: MUTABLE
SYMBOL: "M" WITH ITS TAIL
    CURVING BENEATH IT

Virgos are the zodiac's Nature Kids. Born at harvest time, these earth signs know that it takes patience and hard work to help projects and pals ripen to perfection. Ruler Mercury, the planet of smarts, gives fast talk, fleet feet, and a genius for problem-solving to these mutable marvels.

The horoscope's chief healer offers lots of down-to-earth help. And you bring a breath of fresh air to this modest amigo, inviting Virgo into your whirlwind of friends and fun. Best of all, both you smarties are kind and tactful and loaded with facts and info.

Star Wars? While this picky pal plots and plans, you run screaming, "Dullsville!" If the criticism bugs you, remember, Virgo just wants pals to be perfect. (And wouldn't that be nice…?)

47

LIBRA FRIENDS

DATES: SEPTEMBER 23–OCTOBER 23
SIGN OF THE BALANCE
RULER: VENUS
ELEMENT: AIR
QUALITY: CARDINAL
SYMBOL: THE SCALES

Libra's symbol are the scales of justice, truth, and harmony. Something unfair? These kids cry "foul!" Ruled by Venus, Libras need beauty—ugly places drive them nuts. But don't call these chatty air signs wimps! They keep iron fists tucked inside their velvet gloves.

You two air signs hang-glide to the fun. The Talk Show Host is bewitched by your awesome ideas and care for causes—if only Libra could commit to one thing! And you're awed by Libra's classy tact and passion for pairing off. This is one superbo duo.

Star Wars? That flattery! You eat it up till you realize Libra dishes it out to everyone. And each time you leap toward the next hip idea, Libra dawdles over options. But don't toss this valuable friendship to the winds; you have lots to learn from Libra!

SCORPIO FRIENDS

Dates: October 24–November 23
Sign of the Scorpion
Ruler: Pluto
Element: Water
Quality: Fixed
Symbol: "M" with
    scorpion's tail

Ruled by Pluto, planet of the underworld, Scorpios are magicians: They can turn the hairiest mishaps into lucky events. These water signs focus their psychic radar on you with fixed-quality determination. When these Sherlocks finally give the thumbs-up, expect lifelong loyalty.

Hang with the super sleuth, and count on a meeting of the zodiac's fastest minds. (That underwater radar is speedy!) Your wide-open nature helps Scorpio kick back and trust. Meanwhile, this true-blue cohort reminds you to keep mum when finishing special projects.

Star Wars? Scorpio's secrets make breezy Water Bearer nervous. One wrong move and out comes the Scorpio stinger. But keep cool with Scorp, since this friendship is fixed (like your signs) in the stars.

SAGITTARIUS FRIENDS

DATES: NOVEMBER 24–
   DECEMBER 22
SIGN OF THE ARCHER
RULER: JUPITER
ELEMENT: FIRE
QUALITY: MUTABLE
SYMBOL: THE ARROW

Ruled by jolly Jupiter, this flaming fire sign's motto is "More, More, More!" Mutable Archers shoot their arrows at all sorts of goals. And thanks to their optimism, these Shooting Stars often get bull's-eyes. But don't mistake these happy-go-lucky kids for clowns—Sadges are quick learners and natural teachers.

You high-spirited Two Musketeers are both firm believers in the future! Sadge loves your ability to round up a group of pals in seconds flat. And this boisterous buddy is always ready to act on your big, bold dreams. Talk about a sun-sign sensation.

Star Wars? The blunt honesty. Poor Sadge doesn't know how much those arrows of truth can sting. But you can always depend on this straight shooter for free-wheeling fun and a world-class friendship.

CAPRICORN FRIENDS

DATES: DECEMBER 23–JANUARY 21
SIGN OF THE SEA-GOAT
RULER: SATURN
ELEMENT: EARTH
QUALITY: CARDINAL
SYMBOL: HORNS OF THE
   GOAT, TAIL OF THE FISH

See the tip-top of the zodiac? Hardworking Capricorns have even scaled the horoscope with their steady climb. They might be ruled by stern Saturn, but these down-to-earth kids can be ha-ha hilarious. Don't expect to see Caps trotting off in wacky directions. Why should they? It's a nice view from the top.

Aquarius and Cap respect each other. The zodiac's *Cap*tain seeks excellence and pushes you to do your best, too. Meanwhile, you bring a breath of fresh air to this pal. You two are an unstoppable team.

Star Wars? Capricorn can play Billy Goat Gruff to your brilliant brainstorms. A secret: Confident Cap is less likely to go out on a ledge than you. Just lend your friendly moxie and enjoy this top-notch pal.

AQUARIUS FRIENDS

DATES: JANUARY 22–FEBRUARY 19
SIGN OF THE WATER BEARER
RULER: URANUS
ELEMENT: AIR
QUALITY: FIXED
SYMBOL: WAVES OF WATER

Expect the unexpected. Aquarians are stubborn freethinkers. These air signs (not airheads) are powered by Uranus, planet of ideas and sudden change. And as fixed kids they're no strangers to hard work and discipline. Sounds like a recipe for achievement!

Look alive, Water Bearer! Alliance with another Shock Jock keeps you on your toes. You love this pal's independence and powerful brain (just like uranium!). Aquarius relaxes when listening to your snazzy schemes, and treats your dilemmas with heavenly logic. And wherever you go, a crowd soon gathers for rad fun.

Star Wars? You're both pros at finding the truth. But what if you don't agree? (Could become a fixed—like cement—dilemma.) Good thing you two admire each other. Stick together for state-of-the-art fun!

PISCES FRIENDS

DATES: FEBRUARY 20–MARCH 20
SIGN OF THE FISH
RULER: NEPTUNE
ELEMENT: WATER
QUALITY: MUTABLE
SYMBOL: TWO FISH

Pisces are the zodiac's Dreamboats. Like their symbol of two fish swimming in opposite directions, these water signs are slightly divided. Being mutable, they keep their options open. Neptune adds a wild imagination and glamorous glow.

You're inspired by Fish's endless creativity, and delighted by the famous faith in friendship. (Nobody's a better listener than Pisces.) Meanwhile, Fish is dazzled by your crackerjack insights and sense of fair play. You two artists soar (and swim) together.

Star Wars? Breaking a fingernail or losing a tennis ball ruins Pisces' month. And Fish swims away fast when those sea-deep feelings are hurt. But this friendship stays afloat when you tune into the watery wavelength. Bon voyage!

SIGNS OF LOVE

You fall in love (or will someday) in the same way you do everything else—with air-sign cool. Why go overboard when you're an Aquarius? Your sweetheart is a friend first. As for the flowers and moonlight, well, you'd rather dream up plans for future fun. And if your crush calls every day, or expects you to, you lose interest at the speed of lightning. Freedom first for the Shock Jock!

Usually there's a long line of fans waiting to hold hands with Aquarius. Here's a glimpse at how your romances might shape up along the zodiac trail.

ARIES: Great balls of fire! You adore the Ram's honesty, courage, and charisma. You two could be the hippest couple at school. But sometimes Aries wants you to commit only to Aries—no way! Still, this fiery flirtation is sure fun. The Perfect Plan: A sports event.

TAURUS: The Bull listens up to your plots and plans and, in return, gives you support and grounding when you're frazzled. Don't you feel safe around your Taurus beloved? Any problems? Well, maybe it gets too safe. The Perfect Plan: A nature walk, while sharing snacks.

GEMINI: Count on the Quicksilver Kid to double your fun. You two are the original plugged-in pair, if this witty wonder isn't juggling several sweethearts. The Perfect Plan: Trip to an amusement park, or just hanging at the corner magazine rack.

CANCER: Most days you like being smothered by the best cuddler in the zodiac. But beware hurting this moon-ruled homebody's feelings, or watch the Crab scuttle away. The Perfect Plan: Hanging out at home, especially if cooking's involved.

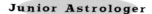

LEO: Talk about fiery romance! Your instant attraction to your opposite sign can last. But don't step on the pride of the Sunshine Kid, or you'll be the one burning. The Perfect Plan: A party where Leo can make a grand entrance.

VIRGO: Thoughtful Virgo is awed by your bold exploits and humdinger ideas. And all that thinking is fun for you—talk about brains in love! You spur Virgo to fun and action. The Perfect Plan: A mega-bookstore where you can explore, read, and stop for sodas.

LIBRA: There's an easy attraction to this fellow air sign. You move forward with talk and plans, while Venus-ruled Libra shows you what romance is all about. Libra is clingier than Aquarius, yes, but you always learn from this partner. The Perfect Plan: Painting, dancing, or shopping for clothes.

SCORPIO: The Scorpio is as strong-willed as you, making for major intrigue. Sure, the secretiveness gets on your nerves, and forget the jealousy. But Scorp runs the zodiac's department of mysterious attraction, so you might be hooked. The Perfect Plan: An afternoon of brainteasers and games.

SAGITTARIUS: Sadge likes anything that involves exploring new horizons and a lot of laughs. When you two take the high road, you're never bored. Somehow, you always end up planning for future fun! The Perfect Plan: A bus trip downtown.

CAPRICORN: Going steady is exactly what you and this clever earth sign do—climbing the mountaintop of romance at an even pace. But is the gait slow for you? The Perfect Plan: Hiking outdoors, or strolling a bookstore's aisles.

AQUARIUS: This pairing is exciting, once you let a fellow Shock Jock rock your world. But don't bother trying to pin this free-thinking wanderer down. You both enjoy time on your own. The Perfect Plan: A trip to a busy game arcade at the mall.

PISCES: When it comes to romance, the Dreamboat is a loveboat. Fish is much more bashful than you—but oh, that haze of glamour! You treasure time spent figuring out the Pisces puzzle. The Perfect Plan: Feeding the ducks, or making arts and crafts at home.

AQUARIUS ALL GROWN UP

You were born to change the world. Not every Shock Jock grows up to be scientist Charles Darwin or talk show host Oprah Winfrey, but you won't rest until you pour your wisdom and understanding on others. And never fear—your bright enthusiasm for new ideas will attract success.

Here's a list of things that keep Aquarius career-happy:

CREATIVITY: You'll always be ahead of your time, bringing cutting edge ideas to the office.

REVOLUTION: Aquarius can always find room for change. (You are determined to make the world a better place, after all.)

IMPROVEMENT: If you aren't fighting off eco-villains to control pollution, you'll make sure your company is recycling.

CHALLENGE: You'll never be satisfied with a downhill sleighride through life. You use your brains and will power to battle to the airy heights.

ORGANIZATION: Your notions may be way out, but your system is well in line. Whatever field you enter, you set up smart step-saving plans.

INDEPENDENCE: You might end up as your own boss. In any case, you'll need plenty of free reign to make your world-class notions come true.

TRADITIONAL AQUARIUS FIELDS

- Astrology
- Entertainment: movies, singing
- Flight: airplanes, rockets
- Hairdressing
- Hi-tech communications: computers, telephones
- Invention
- Party planning
- Political reform
- Psychology, counseling, social work
- Science: astronomy
- Writing: advertising, broadcasting, publishing

AQUARIUS HALL OF FAME

"Why sometimes I believe as many as six impossible things before breakfast."
—Lewis Carroll, mathematician and writer

Each of these Aquarians achievers made the most of his or her star-given talents.

Susan B. Anthony *(social activist)*
George Balanchine *(choreographer)*
Mikhail Baryshnikov *(ballet dancer)*
Judy Blume *(writer)*
Humphrey Bogart *(actor)*
Lord Byron *(poet)*
Anton Chekhov *(writer, playwright, physician)*
Colette *(novelist, actor)*
Sam Cooke *(singer, songwriter, producer)*
James Dean *(actor, icon)*
Charles Dickens *(novelist)*
Frederick Douglass *(abolitionist, journalist, orator)*
Thomas Alva Edison *(inventor)*
Galileo Galilei *(astronomer, physicist, mathematician)*
Phillip Glass *(avante-garde composer)*
Wayne Gretzky *(hockey player)*

Aquarius

Matt Groening (*cartoonist, creator,* The Simpsons)
Hadrian (*world-conquering Roman emperor*)
Etta James (*singer*)
Abraham Lincoln (*U.S. president, freed the slaves*)
Charles Lindbergh (*legendary aviator*)
Bob Marley (*reggae singer, songwriter*)
Toni Morrison (*Nobel Prize-winning novelist*)
Wolfgang Amadeus Mozart (*master composer*)
Paul Newman (*actor, philanthropist*)
Thomas Paine (*American revolutionary leader, writer*)
Anna Pavlova (*ballerina*)
Jackson Pollock (*action painter*)
Mary Lou Retton (*champion gymnast*)
Jackie Robinson (*first African-American major league
  baseball player, baseball legend*)
Franklin Delano Roosevelt (*U.S. president*)
Babe Ruth (*baseball legend*)
Gertrude Stein (*poet, writer*)
Laura Ingalls Wilder (*children's writer*)
Chuck Yeager (*astronaut, test pilot*)

GALACTIC GIFT GUIDE

ARIES likes anything new: Hats, model cars, tools, sports gear. Colors: Red, white, and see-through.

The best gifts for **TAURUS** show good taste or taste good: Cookies, socks, plants. Colors: All shades of green.

Make it fun—like **GEMINI.** Pick games, joke books, or magic tricks. Colors: Orange—anything bright!

A card and a photo of you two, antiques, pillows, or food is perfect for **CANCER.** Colors: Anything silvery or shimmery.

Take **LEO** out! Also: Movie tickets, CDs, hair accessories. Colors: Gold, red, orange, and yellow.

For **VIRGO** keep it simple and neat: All-natural products, how-to books, computer games. Colors: Yellow-green, earthy colors, and white.

The best gift for **LIBRA** is your company. Also: Music, books, flowers, clothes, and sweets. Colors: Mauve and pastels; red for special days.

Slip **SCORPIO** the gift on the sly, or have a treasure hunt for a detective book, a magic or science kit, or art supplies. Colors: Maroon, deep blue, and green.

Bring **SADGE** to a room full of rowdies. Try tickets to a game, maps, and sci-fi stuff. Colors: Purple, royal blue, white, and anything Day-Glo.

Appeal to **CAP'S** big goals: A pen set, biographies of famous folks, helium balloons. Colors: Navy blue, earth tones, and silver.

AQUARIUS likes science experiments, high-tech gear, anything striped—just make sure it's a surprise! Colors: Sky blue, shocking blue or yellow, even neon.

PISCES wants magic. Snatch up a book of poetry, pictures, sunglasses, or candles. Colors: Pale blue-green, white, silver, and purple.

AMAZING THINGS WILL HAPPEN TO YOU!